MW00612932

Dog Packing
in National Parks

How a Pack Dog Became a Service Dog

Jane Cox

Dog Packing in National Parks:
How a Pack Dog Became a Service Dog

Published by Cross Country Publications
Post Office Box 3369
Central Point, OR 97502-0014
Orders: crosscountrypub@cybernetisp.net

Copyright © 2003 by Jane G. Cox
Cover photo and design by Lyle Trimmer

All rights reserved. No part of this book may be reproduced or transmitted by any means, electronic or mechanical, including photocopying, recording, or by any storage and retrieval system, without written permission from the author, except for the inclusion of brief quotations in a review.

Although the author and publisher have researched all available sources at the time of this writing, government rules, regulations and individual park policies are subject to change. The author assumes no responsibility for errors, inaccuracies, omissions, or any inconsistencies herein. Readers should use their own judgment and get current professional advice from the applicable agency, or field of expertise as it applies to their specific situation.

Cox, Jane G.

Dog packing in national parks: how a pack dog became a service dog / Jane Cox. — Central Point, OR : Cross Country Publications, 2003.

p. ; cm.

ISBN: 0-9725393-0-1

1. Service dogs. 2. Animals as aids for people with disabilities. 3. People with disabilities—Recreation. 4. People with disabilities—Orientation and mobility. 5. National parks and reserves—United States.

HV1569.6.C69 2003   2002095206
636.73—dc21   CIP

Table of Contents

Appendix

Preface

Many people I met while hiking in national parks with my service/pack dog enjoyed seeing a dog on the trail, missed their dog at home, or had questions about service/pack dogs. This book is about how one pack dog became a service dog when his person declared her right to hike with a service/pack dog in the backcountry of national parks.

I share with you some of Trigger's formative months to illustrate the importance of the temperament, education and guided exposure that any dog needs to be dependable and steady in a variety of unpredictable and unusual outdoor situations. I talk about trail manners for dogs, and the importance of showing consideration and respect for other travelers.

There are chapters about the preparation, conditioning and planning necessary for a high elevation backcountry adventure with your canine companion. I discuss The Americans With Disabilities Act and the legal challenges of traveling with a service dog. There are some questions for thought on the future of dog packing in national parks. I have written this book so that others may benefit from my research and experience.

This book is dedicated to the many people I met on the trail who gave encouragement and asked questions about how it was possible to have a dog on a trail in a national park. You are my inspiration for this book, and this book is for you.

Acknowledgements

My special thanks go out to Tom Coleman, Recreation Access Specialist, National Park Service, Park Facility Management Division, Washington D. C.; Shawn Costello, Superintendent of Concession Services in Yosemite National Park, and all the park supervisors, corridor rangers, and camp staff in Yosemite and the Grand Canyon for making my travels a most enjoyable and memorable experience.

Also to Mark Earnest who helped me through the computer formatting issues and editing tasks.

1

On the Trail

"Is he something special, or just a mutt?" the man asked, as I passed him on the trail. Trigger, my 65 pound Australian Shepherd mix stood beside me with tail wagging, ready, as always, to meet this inquisitive stranger with the blunt question of parentage.

With a service dog, I was very aware that Trigger and I had the responsibility to set a good example and to educate people about service dogs in national parks. Often when we stepped off the trail for a break, or to let people pass, we got questions and I always took the time to answer them as accurately as possible. A lot of questions were about service dogs:

What kind of service does he perform?
(Trigger standing there with his pack on.)

Did he go to service dog school?

Where do you <u>get</u> a pack dog?

While many dogs are trained by professionals and there are schools for the most common functions that dogs perform, such as guide and sound alert, many more dogs are trained by owners to perform the services necessary to meet their own unique specific needs. The broad definition, according to Title 3 of the Americans With Disabilities Act is:

> Service animals include any animal individually trained to do work or perform tasks for the benefit of an individual with a disability.

When I adopted Trigger I didn't know he was to become my service/pack dog. But as our relationship developed and his training progressed, I also learned that I qualified under the Americans With Disabilities Act (ADA) to declare him as my service/pack dog. This makes it possible for me to take him into national parks and other places where dogs as pets are not allowed.

Laura, age ten, asked "Does he turn lights on and off for you?" "No, but I taught him to open the door for himself when he wants to go outside. I have a strap tied to the door knob for him to pull it open, and it swings shut behind him." There are many things that I have taught Trigger to do because he keeps "asking to be taught." In Trigger's case, he is happiest when he feels useful.

If you hike with a service dog, one personal question that you should be prepared to deal with is the obvious one: Why do you need a service dog? The details and nature of your response may depend on who is asking and why. While the ADA does not require you to show proof of your restriction, you should inform park superintendents that you qualify under the ADA for canine pack carrying assistance, so that they can notify their corridor rangers of this policy exception. You should not be asked to show specific medical documentation, although they may ask the nature of your disability.

Most people do not understand how an individual can hike five or six miles over mountainous terrain and be disabled. When I meet people in the high mountain camps or on the trail I tell them about the ADA that mandates a much more user-friendly (though relatively untested) definition of disability than that of the federal government for a Social Security disability grant. The ADA uses the terms "restriction", "limitation", and "impairment" all interchangeably with the word "disabled." I don't consider myself disabled by Social Security standards; I am substantially limited in what I can carry. (See Chapter four for a more in-depth discussion of the ADA). The purpose of the ADA is to ensure that people with limitations are not denied full and equal enjoyment of the "goods, services, facilities, privileges, advantages or accommodations" offered by a place of public service.

By and large all the people I met were openly supportive of what I was doing. Michael and Marta, fellow hikers of the high country in Yosemite, became special friends. Michael saw us at Tuolumne Meadows in Yosemite on the first day of our hut to hut trek there, and made a special point of saying how happy he was to see that I could hike with my dog. They, like others we met missed their own dogs at home and wanted to know how they could bring them into the park.

At this time, only dogs performing a needed function to compensate for a physical (or mental) limitation of its handler can accompany its person on trails in national parks.

2
Growing Up

I am an enthusiastic and active outdoor person who has hiked, backpacked and cross-country skied all my life. Living without a dog was not easy. I always missed not having one when my living or work situation prevented me from providing a good home for a dog. But when I retired and got my own home, Trigger came into my life. On about my third visit to the pound I saw him there, an Australian Shepherd mix, in a concrete and chain link kennel with his mom, littermates, a small blanket and a bowl of water. Most all of the dogs were clamoring for attention, but Trigger was off to one side watching his brothers and sisters play. His bright brown eyes were framed by copper eyebrows and cheeks, black merled ears, and just enough brindled gray across his muzzle to set off a generous sprinkling of black "freckles." He appeared to be alert and interested, but also calm and thoughtful.

I asked for an attendant to help me get him out. When I did so I spoke to his mom. She did not try to leave the kennel or prevent me from taking her puppy. I will never forget how she looked into my eyes and gave a mournful little howl of resignation.

I was able to put Trigger down on the floor in the food preparation area to give him a quick puppy response test to assess his degree of attraction to people, his desire to follow, and to see how he reacted to restraint and canine domination signals. In spite of all the pots banging and confusion, he appeared to be confident, in the mid range of assertiveness, and he did not hesitate to come to me and follow me around.

Part of the adoption process included a physical check-up. The vet who examined him said he was of normal development, healthy, and about seven weeks old. She also was impressed by his calm nature. From the moment I brought him home he seemed to accept and appreciate everything I did for him, from the flea baths to nursing him through Parvovirus, which he came down with the day after I brought him home. The vet said he wasn't sick enough to have Parvo, but sadly, I later got a call from the pound warning me that his mother had proven to be a carrier of Parvo and had passed it on to her puppies. They all had to be destroyed. Needless to say I changed vets.

I slept on the floor by Trigger's kennel every night till he was out of danger. I syringe fed him baby food and Pedialyte® (water and electrolyte replacement for babies). I knew he was past the crisis when he wagged his tail and eagerly accepted nourishment.

When Trigger was fully recovered I took him walking with me on trails and in parks near where I live. He was the center of his own brand new universe, and he drew me into his world of wonderment. He would stuff his nose into a gopher hole, or spring straight up in the air to pounce on a grasshopper with all the confidence and conviction of an experienced and fearless hunter. He reminded me that nature is an eternal adventure just waiting to happen. Training was always fun for him because it was part of our walks.

After he learned all the basic commands on leash he graduated to a six-foot dragline tied to his collar for off leash training. During the initial part of this transition period he did lots of close heeling, sits, stays and comes. He learned to do random "sits" away from my side. If ever he didn't come the first time I called him, he was on leash

"What do you mean I can't run down the trail?"

for the remainder of the walk. No scolding or punishment, just quiet, matter of fact, cause and effect. I used every potential distraction as a training opportunity. The reward for coming promptly was praise, sometimes a treat, and immediate release to continue under voice control. He soon learned that responsible behavior was rewarded with his most valued privilege— supervised freedom.

I tried to anticipate everything that could possibly go wrong, and take steps to avoid any possible negative outcome. Once when Trigger was a puppy we were walking through an open wooded area and he got the "crazies", as puppies sometimes do. I knew the worst thing I could do would be to call him or try to catch him. He was wild-eyed and running in big circles around me.

Before he was trained to recall I never played chase games with Trigger, because I knew I couldn't win. From a dog's point of view, if he (1) initiates the game of chase, (2) you chase him, and (3) he wins, then (4) he must be the leader! I waited a minute and he was still acting crazy so I sat down on a log, made myself as small as I could, and hid my face in my hands. It was very hard for me to ignore him, and I had no idea if it would work. But very soon, curiosity got the best of him and he came over to investigate. I slowly reached over to pet him and hooked my fingers around his collar. No big deal, for <u>him</u>! We continued our walk on leash. That was scary for me, because even though he was in no immediate danger I had not anticipated what I would do in that kind of situation. He never had the "crazies" like that, either before or after that incident.

This method works best with dogs that have a bonded relationship with the trainer and have been set up for lots of successes and no negative experiences in their formative training, including great (from the dog's point of view) escapes!

3
Working Together

Because training was fun for Trigger, he always looked to me for directions, and seemed to beg for new challenges and "stuff" to learn. So I taught him all the useful trail commands I could think of, such as "off the trail" (when people approach), ahead, behind and wait. Then we moved on to long distance hand signals (down, stay, come, sit), and seek-backs: "Trigger, I dropped my keys; would you go find them for me please?" It has become harder and harder to set them down quietly so that he won't notice; he often knows when I am about to do this.

Other commands that come in handy sometimes are "go to the car" (taught with a treat on or by the vehicle), and "go to the tent." He can lead me right to it in the dark.

Trail training would not be complete without careful desensitization to lots of distractions—people, other dogs, bicycles, horses and mules.

This is where the command "off the trail" is very useful. Trigger sits beside the trail until released.

Positive training techniques inspire eager and enthusiastic responses as demonstrated In this seek-back exercise.

When he was tempted to chase a squirrel I used a long distance "sit" in place rather than a recall to keep him from chasing anything that he saw close by. Better to use an immobilizing command, such as "sit" or "down" rather than an active command when his predatory reflexes are tempted. I don't expect a young dog to give me a flawless recall when a squirrel runs across his path. I used the dragline for backup to have him sit in place. Then he could be rewarded for a steady response.

Trigger has camped enough with me that he has developed a good sense of what is normal activity and what is unusual. When he was only about six months old he "woofed" at something in the middle of the night. I listened for a minute, heard nothing and told him to be quiet. Less than five minutes later an owl hooted in a tree just above our tent. A large owl could carry off a small dog. Another night he "woofed" at something in the meadow close to our tent. Again, in all my superior human intelligence I told him to be quiet, nothing was there. Within the hour we were serenaded by the bugling of elk close by. Trigger doesn't bark at many things, but now when he does, I trust his judgment. His alarm barks are, if anything, understated. (I thought he never would let me know when someone comes to the door, but he finally did start to do that consistently when he was about three years old.)

Other activities we engage in, such as attending horse shows at fair grounds and canine agility, practiced in a horse arena, give him exposure and training to reinforce his steady behavior around livestock and in distracting environments. He has been tested and approved for participation in Delta Society's Pet Partner Program, and we volunteer at a hospital and in a school as a pet therapy team.

Trigger carries a pack for me when I cross country ski, which offers its own set of special challenges.

It takes a well-trained dog to stay out of the way and to follow various voice commands. Once we were skiing at Diamond Lake in southern Oregon, when a dog sled team came running up the road straight toward us! The lead dog swerved just as he got to within a few feet. There was an Iditerod training run at the resort that weekend. I'm sure that Trigger's adrenaline was rushing, as was mine, but he sat steady until I released him.

As for myself, when I was hiking up to twelve miles a day, and going on self contained extended backpacks I was usually in a wilderness area or other inaccessible (by car) or difficult (by foot) place to reach. I thought national parks would be fun to visit when I could no longer carry a full pack—sometime in the far distant future.

Well, I have entered a new phase in my life. That future is here and Trigger carries my pack when I go on day hikes or cross country ski tours. Now, instead of backpacking I like to hike between established camps where meals and primitive shelter are provided.

The problem is, now that I am retired and have a life style where both dog and outdoors are so much a part of my life they are inseparable, I find that only guide dogs can go out of developed areas in national parks.

4

Logistics

Could I possibly be eligible to hike with my dog under the Americans With Disabilities Act (ADA)? First, I requested a copy of the ADA from the Department of Justice (DOJ). General eligibility criteria in the DOJ 28 Code of Federal Regulations, Part 36.301 states: "a public accommodation shall not impose or apply eligibility criteria that screen out or tend to screen out an individual with a disability or any class of individuals with disabilities from fully and equally enjoying any goods, services, facilities, privileges, advantages or accommodations....being offered."

The act further expands the right of a disabled individual to be allowed modifications in policies, practices, or procedures unless doing so would fundamentally alter the nature of the goods, services, facilities, privileges, advantages, or accommodations (36.302). The ADA uses the terms "disability", "impairment", "restriction", and "limitation" all interchangeably.

The basic definition of disability as stated in the DOJ 28 Code of Federal Regulations (CFR) Part 36.104 is:

> "with respect to an individual, a physical or mental impairment that substantially limits one or more of the major life activities of such individual; a record of such impairment; or being regarded as having such an impairment"

Title II-2.2000 of the Americans With Disabilities Act explains in detail what physical impairments are included, with examples. The ADA website and help line are listed in the appendix. The next step was to consult with my doctor and see a specialist. Each time I went in for an examination or testing I took a copy of the ADA's definition of disability so that the doctor could determine whether (in his opinion) I met the definition of disability under the ADA.

Then I sent this medical information along with a synopsis of my outdoor experience and of Trigger's training and temperament, and of his dependable behavior around people, livestock and other animals, to the National Park Service (NPS) in Washington, D. C. I asked that Trigger be allowed to accompany me in the backcountry of national parks as my service/pack dog.

Soon after I sent that request, the Access Specialist called me and said that all I needed to do was apply at any national park for a disabled pass, and with that Golden Access Passport I should be able to gain permission from individual wilderness managers to hike the back country with my dog in the parks I visited. He sent me a brochure explaining the eligibility criteria for obtaining the Golden Access Passport (GAP) (see appendix).

The NPS expects the bearer of the GAP to have signed an affidavit stating that he meets the same exclusive medical criteria that the Social Security and Veterans Administration require for a financial grant based on disability. In order to get a Golden Access Passport, I was being asked to sign a statement that appeared to me to be misleading and false.

I wrote a letter explaining that I did not meet the Social Security definition of disability because I had never been determined unable to perform any substantial gainful employment of any kind. And I didn't think this was an appropriate statement to be asked to sign because Social Security does not do disability determinations on people who are receiving retirement benefits.

I told them I was retired, able to continue hiking with pack carrying assistance, and wanted to qualify to bring my dog into the park under the new <u>inclusive</u> ADA medical criteria. The access specialist responded with a phone call and assured me that the park service is only trying to ascertain whether the individual meets the definition of "an individual with a disability" as established by Section 504 and the ADA. They ask for documentation from a medical source confirming the disability, or if the person does not have such documentation, they simply ask them to sign a legal statement attesting to the fact that the applicant has "a physical, sensory, or motor impairment that severely limits one or more major life activities." He told me that the only way to become accepted for recognition under the ADA was to sign the Golden Access Passport application, declaring medical eligibility for a federal disability grant.

So, with all our documentation in hand I drove up to my local national park. I presented all this to the official at the desk, expecting to have a lengthy discussion, probably culminating in a call to the access specialist in Washington. But no! It was too easy. The park ranger just handed me the affidavit to sign and didn't want any documentation. Still not wanting to misrepresent myself or run into any problems miles from home at a national park later, I left my statements anyway, asking that they be attached to my application.

Just minutes after I got home I got a call from the park superintendent stating that they had issued the disability pass in error, and that I must return it. I referred him to the access specialist, and soon after, the park superintendent called again to apologize, saying everything was OK, and wouldn't I stop in and "chat" with him the next time I was in his park? (Hmm---) I graciously accepted his apology and said I would. If I had not talked to the access specialist I would never have signed the Golden Access Passport application.

Ostensibly the Federal Government is not even covered by the ADA. The Rehabilitation Act of 1973 is the document that was provided to ensure disability rights for employees within the Federal Government, and Section 504 was later added to include all individuals participating in any federal program, such as visitors to national parks. The Rehabilitation Act of 1973 was written twenty-five years ago, and Congress has never revised the "Federal Recreation Passport Program" brochure to expand the options independent of Social Security for proving eligibility under the ADA. So the government still excludes all those people who would potentially meet the ADA's less restrictive definition of disability. The ADA states that whichever law is least restrictive, will take precedence over the other. So, in the end the ADA will prevail if it is less restrictive than the Rehabilitation Act. The ADA was patterned after the Rehabilitation Act.

Even after showing the Golden Access Passport I am still stopped and (or) warned by some park rangers. More on this in Chapter Twelve. At the time I last checked, the CFRs still do not contain any official and complete disability policy that is in compliance with the ADA.

5

Preparing for Backcountry Travel

Hiking in alpine conditions is not just a walk in the park. You are often hours, if not days, away from your car, a road, and other people. It is important to have the right amount of gear to be prepared for emergencies, but not overloaded. You must also have the skills and experience necessary to get yourself safely from your starting point to your destination on a trail you may never have seen before. Having a map and compass won't do any good if you don't know how to use them together. This book isn't about learning to be self-sufficient in the outdoors, except to stress the importance of being a competent wilderness traveler before you make your dog a full risk-taking partner. There are some good books on backpacking and dog packing listed in the bibliography. Carefully assess the needs, wants and capabilities of both you and your partner before you head into the wilderness. Be sure to read *Ruffing It* before you plan your trip.

If you are an experienced outdoor person, and you have a sturdy, well-behaved dog, he has the potential to be of substantial help to you. Initially you have a willing partner, and you don't want to get him all loaded down, half way to your destination, with feet too sore to go any further.

The first thing I think of for myself is adequate foot care and protection. This is especially important for a pack-carrying dog. You may think his feet are fairly tough, but you should still have leather booties for him. High elevation trails above timberline are often on sharp and exposed rock, which can get very hot. Even sand gets hotter at lower temperatures at high elevations. Long stretches of shale and lava rock would be hard on a dog's feet, even without the weight of a pack.

You can make the booties yourself, or buy them from a large pet store or dog supply catalog. Get them or make them early enough to make sure they stay on his feet, offer insulation from heat, and have non-slip soles. I don't like Cordura pack cloth for booties because it is too hot to wear in the summer and is slippery on smooth surfaces. Most insulated boots are made for winter use. There is a sketch in the appendix for leather booties. Leather will stretch and mold to his feet, so they should fit snugly or they will flop around at the toe. A Velcro band should fasten just above where his foot starts to flare out. Make the booties several months before you go so they can be worn enough for the dog to get used to them and so you have plenty of time to fit them properly. Booties don't stay on very well when they get wet, so I remove them for stream crossings and water breaks.

My dog doesn't wear his booties all the time. They are a nuisance if not needed. The important thing is to always be aware of how your dog is walking. If he runs from shady spot to shady spot, or wants to stand in one, that's a clue. If he holds one of his feet up high, the ground is too hot. Feel the tread surface occasionally if it is exposed; the heat it radiates may surprise you. Put on his boots when you come to a long rocky stretch, before he has a problem. When he carries a pack, his front feet are going to take a beating, especially going down hill.

Examine your friend's feet carefully at the end of each day. One afternoon when I took his pack off, and he had rested, I was walking with him through camp and he just lay down and didn't want to go any further. I wasn't surprised that he was tired, because I was too. But when I examined his feet carefully, he had some pitch between his pads with small, sharp grit stuck to it. I removed the pitch with some mosquito repellent oil and

Trigger's toothbrush. Then I scrubbed his foot to get out any pitch and oil residue with warm soapy water and (you guessed it) his toothbrush. I was relieved to find that he seemed to enjoy the foot massage and was fine after that. It helps to be part nurse, part detective, and a lot creative when you travel with your dog and just the bare essentials. My favorite light oil for removing pitch is Avon's Skin-So-Soft, but I didn't have that with me. Trimming the hair between his pads just before you leave is a good idea, especially if he has long hair; and trim his nails regularly, as you can only cut a little off at one time.

Watch how your dog walks after he has rested, and again the next morning. If he shows any signs of being foot sore, start out with his booties, at least on his front (weight bearing) feet. You should include in his pack a roll of vet tape and some antibiotic spray for both you and the dog. An Ace® bandage could come in handy for either one of you.

When hiking, you will be safer and more comfortable if you don't have to hold onto a leash. I made a light-weight nylon tether with a sliding snap buckle at each end long enough to fasten around my waist and allow a full stride between my dog's back feet and my forward foot when I am walking. The other end of the leash snaps into a "D" ring sewn to the back edge of the dog pack. I found that when Trigger walked in front, the leash often hooked around the front of the pack when it was fastened to his collar. I usually have him walk ahead of me when walking up hill and behind when going down.

If you are camping at high elevations, temperatures can easily drop below freezing at night, even in the summer. A warm coat and an Ensolite® pad for your dog is a must. One morning after a very cold night in the Grand Canyon, I promised Trigger that on our next trip he would have a warm sleeping coat. It was so cold, when I spilled a few drops of water they froze before they hit the table, and little chickadees were right there as soon as they hit, trying to pry them loose! In the desert, water is even more precious than food. Ravens pecked holes in my plastic water jug when I was away from camp for a few minutes.

The cabin tents in Yosemite were on concrete foundations so I put a piece of a space blanket under the Ensolite® pad to reflect my dog's body heat back to him. It hardly takes up any space, and weighs practically nothing.

Your dog is burning lots of calories and working hard for you in the daytime; and it takes more energy to work and stay warm at higher altitudes.

You may think that a dog coat is unnecessary, but if you do any winter or high elevation camping it is a very good idea. I made Trigger's coat with two layers of polar fleece sandwiched between two layers of coated rip-stop nylon. Trigger only needs his coat at nighttime but some slender, short-coated dogs may need them to stay warm on cold days.

You can make or buy such things as a coated nylon water and food dish. A cut-off plastic Clorox jug holds a good supply of water for overnight camping. Slipped over the end of a bedroll it takes no space, is semi flexible but rigid, and weighs nothing. Don't forget to take 15% to 25% extra food for him, and some trail treats for rest stops.

I have a special tag I add to Trigger's collar when we travel that has my vehicle make, model, color, and license number on it. If you lose your dog on a camping trip you don't want him to be picked up and taken miles away to an animal shelter. Most people would be willing to wait by your car until you come back, or at least tie your dog to it. That would be a lot less traumatic for the dog, too.

Trigger's gear also includes a small pin brush and his toothbrush. Chapter six discusses a pack.

6

Planning Ahead and Conditioning

Once I decided to backpack with my dog, many a winter evening was spent studying books and maps to choose an itinerary and get on waiting lists or make reservations, some as much as a year in advance. There is a lottery to decide who will be able to do the hut-to-hut Yosemite high country out of Tuolumne Meadows each year.

Once I received confirmation of my ten-day high country trek, I made a reservation at a resort just outside of Yosemite for the night before, and for the night after my trek. I was given permission to leave my van there while I was in Yosemite. A bear had broken into my van on the previous trip and I was not going to give them a second chance.

When I made the reservation I declared my service dog, but was told that I would be charged a pet-cleaning fee. I explained that under the ADA it was illegal to charge a cleaning fee but the confirmation they sent had the cleaning fee highlighted, and after giving them references and phone numbers for ADA information they canceled my reservation and offered to make one at a higher cost, asked for proof of Trigger's certification as a service dog, my medical information, and said that I could not leave my van there while I hiked. Just about everything they tried to do was out of compliance with the ADA, so I filed a complaint with the Justice Department, and found a different place to stay. It's good to find out about problems before you get there, and much easier to make alternate plans from home. Just because it is illegal for people to charge a pet fee, ask for proof of certification or medical documentation, doesn't mean that these things won't happen. If you travel with a service dog it is important to know your rights and plan ahead as much as possible.

While I am planning my trip, I start filling an envelope with all the information I might need: reservation confirmation, rabies and inoculation records, canine good citizen certificate, and the telephone number of my access specialist in Washington, D.C. All this in case I have trouble getting him accepted as a service dog. I also composed a letter of introduction for any park official who questions me so that they can have something in writing about myself, my dog, legal information on the ADA, and where they can get more information about the ADA from both the Justice Department and the national park access specialists. It is only recently that service dog status is being considered to other than guide (seeing eye) dogs in national parks, and at the time of this writing the new regulations are being finalized.

There is no universally accepted way to certify a service dog, and many service dogs are not certified. Even though it is illegal for anyone to ask for proof of certification—and most people don't know that—I try to have information about the laws regarding service animals. In addition, I try to have other reasonable documentation, such as therapy dog experience and agility training that might help. Trigger wears a patch on his pack that identifies him as a service dog. The park superintendent is (sometimes) the only authority I offer information to regarding his training and experience before I start my trek. Sometimes the superintendent will give me a letter of introduction for other rangers I might meet since it is unusual to have a dog on the trail in a national park. This letter is helpful when rangers along the way question me—as they always do—although all have been friendly and supportive.

Well before each trip, Trigger and I start to condition ourselves to carrying more weight and hike farther. How much weight can a dog carry? The maximum pack weight recommended for a dog is 25% of its body weight; but that doesn't mean that every dog will carry that much. Trigger weighs a slender 65 to 70 pounds, but he doesn't want to carry fifteen pounds. He will willingly carry about thirteen pounds after several months of gradual conditioning. Some heavier boned breeds, such as Malamutes and Newfoundland's can start out with a good size load and work up to maybe a third of their body weight. So structure has something to do with it, and so does the dog's condition before he starts to carry any weight. If your dog has never had an orthopedic exam, now would be a good time for him to have one. Be especially careful of asking breeds more commonly susceptible to hip displasia to carry heavy loads before they are examined.

Most of the time Trigger only carries about seven or eight pounds on a day trip in the wintertime, and less in the summer. So about two months before an extended hiking trip we carry a pound or two extra on a short hike and gradually work each weight increment up to longer and more difficult

Dog packs are positioned on the shoulders to minimize strain on the lower back and hips.

hikes at higher elevations. When he can start out with about thirteen pounds on a six-mile hike with an elevation gain of about 2000 feet I know he is ready for the real thing. Since he carries all the water we drink in a day, his load lightens as we travel.

If the weather is hot, watch for signs of heat exhaustion and let your dog cool off frequently and drink lots of water. Take off his pack and let him get wet if he wants to. If there is a little water left in his dish, I rub it onto his head and ears, and

31

sometimes he wears a wet bandanna. Choose the cooler days to work hard, especially if you can't get to the higher, cooler elevations for conditioning.

Before you can condition your dog you need to choose a pack. There are books listed in the appendix for fitting and buying a dog pack.

A dog pack is fitted so that it rides on the shoulders, not in the middle of the back; and the dog should be able to lie down comfortably with it on. Books on backpacking with your dog, listed in the bibliography, go into more detail on choosing and loading a dog pack. Chapter five talks about other equipment for your dog.

7

Some People Don't Like Dogs

Some people don't like dogs; and they don't want to be around them or where they have been. While we can't be responsible for feelings that were shaped by past experiences, we can respect those feelings and show that we are friendly and considerate. Most objections people have to dogs are valid and real.

They are allowed to defecate on or near the trail, in campsites, and near water. Pick up after your dog, and toilet him away from where people congregate or are likely to walk.

They are allowed to approach people or enter campsites uninvited. They may be looking for food, or maybe they are just being friendly. No matter. Don't let a dog approach people on his own. People will ask you if they want to pet him.

Some people are afraid of dogs. Fear is one of several healthy responses to a new and possibly threatening situation. We have a choice to either avoid fearful circumstances or deal with them in a pro-active way. As a responsible dog owner it is up to me to be sensitive to the special needs that other people might have. You will get lots of compliments if your dog is trained to sit quietly beside the trail while people pass.

Most of us who camp and backpack are willing to drive miles to escape the noise pollution of the neighborhoods we leave behind. We enjoy the sounds of birds, running water, the wind in the trees and other subtle sounds of nature. Other people camp with generators, chain saws, amplified music and (or) barking dogs. When campers complain to park officials about noise after hours or inconsiderate neighbors, dogs are an easy target. All dog owners are vulnerable to increased restrictions, whether our dogs are well behaved or not. Please take the time to socialize your puppy to accept normal foot traffic close by, sounds of children and other animals. Dogs that bark excessively do not belong in a public campground.

Some people think that dogs should be banned from public land because they may jump on people, bark at or chase animals, and are generally disruptive or incompatible with nature. I have to agree I have seen my share of dogs that are out of bounds and out of control, but contrary to what people may think, a well-trained dog is neither disruptive nor incompatible with nature. Dogs are just as much a part of our natural environment as we humans are. I see more animals when I am with my dog than when I am by myself. Animals aren't any more afraid of a dog than they are of a person, unless they are being stalked or chased.

One afternoon in the campground on the North Rim of the Grand Canyon, Trigger appeared to be asleep, flat out on his side with his eyes closed. Then all of a sudden he was on his feet with his eyes riveted on a tree. Clinging to the opposite side of the tree was a Kaibab Squirrel peeking around the tree trunk at Trigger. The squirrel could certainly have run away or climbed the tree if he wanted to. Trigger could have barked and scared him away. But it was as if time was suspended as two very alert and curious animals contemplated each other. The squirrel was focusing all of his attention on Trigger; and I had the extended opportunity to observe a friendly natural encounter. Trigger is always pointing things out to me, and it's fun to see nature through the eyes of a dog.

At the very least, most people, including dog owners, believe that dogs should always be on leash. I am in the minority in allowing my dog to accompany me off leash whenever the established parameters will allow it. However, when Trigger is off leash I watch him very closely. He must come the first time he is called and have a reliable long distance "sit" and "down" in place. He must respond to my guidance to stay on or near the trail, and he must sit quietly beside the trail when people pass. Because I often carry treats to reward him randomly for prompt responses, he is in the habit of looking to me for directions whenever animals or people are around.

Off leash work is, at best, an intense team effort. It involves concentration and responsibility on the part of both partners. You are the leader of your pack. If you can't give your full attention to supervising your dog, you owe it to yourself, your dog and the public to put him back on leash. We who let our dogs off leash are always under the scrutiny of other hikers and it is up to us to set a good example. My mission is to leave people with the impression of "Maybe there are some responsible dog owners with dogs well enough trained and _supervised_ to be off leash."

If you do have a dog that can be trusted off leash, you have a very special relationship to be treasured, nurtured and enjoyed.

Leashing or tying out your dog is required in national parks at all times.

8
Along the Way in Yosemite

I missed the bus from Crane Flat, at the west entrance to Yosemite into Tuolumne Meadows, where I was to spend my first night. Shawn Costello, Park Supervisor of Concession Services knew I was concerned about the connection before I left home, and said somehow he would get me there if I missed the bus. He didn't yet know what the bus schedule would be for the season, but said to call the transportation desk the day before I would be there, which I did.

My bus into the park got delayed in road construction, and the park shuttle bus driver either wasn't given my message from the day before or he decided not to wait.

When I called the park bus dispatch office I was told that the bus I missed was the only bus of the day, no special consideration could be made and I should hitchhike into Tuolomne Meadows. Someone gave me a scrap of cardboard on which I scratched *Tuolomne Meadows* and stood, with my sign, my dog and two packs where the cars were leaving Crane Flat. People seemed somewhat amused at my plight and it seemed obvious that I wouldn't be getting a ride any time soon.

I had left Shawn's number back in my van at the RV park, but I got it again through Eric, the Crane Flat store manager, who went out of his way to help me. Fortunately, I was able to get Shawn in his office, but it took several conversations to finalize the plans. Eric kept coming out to the parking lot to give me phone calls from Shawn, on his cordless phone. Shawn sent a special van and driver up from the valley to take us into Tuolumne Meadows. There was much time and energy expended by these two people on my behalf, for which I am forever grateful.

But then I got a pang of guilt when the van driver said Shawn thought I was blind. I said, "Oh, I hope he didn't send a van just because he thought I was blind!" Then we both started to laugh. I couldn't imagine myself blind and hitchhiking into Tuolumne Meadows with my pack/guide dog, off to hike the Yosemite High Country. Not that it couldn't be done, but not by me! I thought I was adventurous enough already. Strangely enough, park regulations at the time still stated that only guide dogs were permitted on trails in national parks.

Tuolumne Meadows is a large village of tent cabins around a shower/bathroom and a store/dining room. Most guests drive in, but some take the bus, as I tried to do. From here, (after a short bus ride) access to the other high camps is only by trail.

I sat at a table that night with four businessmen from the east coast, who had flown to San Francisco and rented Harley Davidson motorcycles for a bike tour of the west, from San Francisco to the Grand Canyon. When I saw those Harleys I thought they looked out of place in a national park, but never did I think I would be having dinner with four motorcyclists from New York! One fun thing about visiting national parks is that you will meet people with a variety of interests and from every place on earth! I think they were a little bit impressed that I was hiking the wilderness with just my dog—they said they would never hike into wilderness. I said I don't ride motorcycles either. But it was fun talking to people that I would not otherwise have had a chance to meet. High camp dining rooms are great gathering places for those of us who enjoy independent travel with some amenities.

The next morning I boarded the park shuttle bus which would take us to the trailhead where I would start my seven-day trek. The bus driver got on after I did and said that dogs were not allowed on the bus. We would have to get off. Since Shawn had already helped me get to Tuolumne Meadows, I was confident I could work through this problem. I told the bus driver that Trigger was a service/pack dog, and the rest of the conversation went something like this: "Do you have certification to ride the bus with your dog?" "I have permission from the Wilderness Ranger to hike the back country with him. Here is my letter." "This letter says you can hike with him, not ride my bus. I'm not going anywhere until you get off." "I'm not getting off. I talked to your supervisor before I left home and he said I wouldn't have any trouble riding the bus. Do you want to call him, or shall I?" "I will." When the bus driver came back he didn't say anything and that was the end of the problem. Trigger and I got off the bus at the trailhead to Glen Aulin High Camp.

All of the rangers I met on the trail were supportive and accepting of the fact that Trigger was a service dog, even though they seemed to be confused, because the Code of Federal Regulations still does not conform to the ADA regarding public access for all service dogs.

In Yosemite (as in some other national parks) there are two species of animals that are sacrosanct, one domestic, and the other in an altered wild state. Mules over the years have been a part of the wilderness experience. Visitors have come to depend on them as a means of transportation, and rangers and park staff depend on them as beasts of burden. They are essential for getting food and supplies up to the high camps. The mules are steady and dependable for what they do. The problem is, most of them have never seen dogs.

I was sitting off the trail eating lunch when a string of mules paused to drink from a stream that crossed the trail. It was a potentially tense moment for both dog and mules. The mules all stopped, waiting their turn to drink and turned sideways in the trail to face Trigger, showing all variations of mule surprise, agitation, and curiosity. (They have very expressive faces!) Trigger was lying down, but emitted a slight puppy stress whine, as if to say, "Why are all those mules <u>staring</u> at me?

If you stop for any length of time at all get <u>well</u> off the trail and tie your dog securely in an inconspicuous place. A mule wrangler that might go by will first be startled to see a dog on the trail. Then, (hopefully) notice that he is secured and turn his full attention to avoiding any potential crisis with his mules. Sometimes a mule driver will want you to take your dog out of sight until they pass. It's always a good idea to ask before you approach mules on the trail.

9
Bears!

The wild animal that is especially revered and protected in Yosemite is the black bear. Bears are still part of our natural environment and commonplace in the Pacific Northwest, Canada and Alaska. If you camp much in Yosemite, Yellowstone, Kings Canyon/Sequoia, North Cascades, Glacier or the Olympics it is just a matter of time before you and your dog encounter a bear. Where bears are a problem, the park service is constantly monitoring the camp bear populations, tagging them and observing their behavior, so you are not likely to encounter a bear that has a history of acting aggressively towards people. The park service passes out information instructing people to be sure to remove all their food, gum, toothpaste and cosmetics from their car, and to store it in the metal bear-proof lockers that are usually provided in bear country. Any food smells that linger in your vehicle will attract bears. They say to even store canned food in the lockers because the animals have an excellent sense of smell.

The park service also expects people to take a very active role in preventing bears from stealing food at meal times. If a bear is successful at stealing food the ranger's sympathy seems to go to the bear because the more times an individual bear succeeds at stealing food the more at risk he becomes for destruction. However, if they seem determined to take your pack after you try to scare them off or retreat, let them have it.

On a previous trip to Yosemite, a bear broke into my van one night in Curry Village. I returned to my van the next morning to find that he had popped out a side window, crawled through the opening, and left through the same window with a twenty-five pound bag of dog food. There was not even a scratch on the counter that he (or she) had to crawl over to get under the bench seat where the bag was stored. She knew just what she wanted and she didn't waste any effort. She didn't spill anything. She just left with the groceries.

Because I cook and sleep in my van it would not be practical (or possible) to remove all traces of food and food smells from my vehicle before I leave it over night, so I just don't take it into parks when I am not going to be in it at night time.

The park service used to relocate problem bears but found that it was usually just a matter of time before a relocated bear returned to his old territory. The park service seems to take an excessively tolerant view of bears that steal food and damage property in an attempt to get at it.

There is a refreshingly new, and in my opinion, more direct and sensible approach to bear vandalism. A bear biologist, Carrie Hunt, of Wind River Bear Institute in Utah is teaching problem bears to respect human territory with the help of Karelian Bear Dogs (see Appendix).

Camp bears are very intelligent, strong, and resourceful opportunists that have lost all fear of man. In national parks, where they are protected, they are at the top of the food chain and they think nothing of strolling through a campground at dinnertime, helping themselves to whatever smells and looks good. Trigger saw his first bear in Lodgepole Campground in Sequoia National Park. I heard someone yell "Bear!" across the loop, at which time everyone is supposed to come, yelling and banging on pots and pans to chase the bear away before he gets any food, but it didn't work out that way. The bear chose his dinner one site over from mine, and had just helped himself to one steak on the table and another off the grill, with two men standing there saying "Oh darn bear—go away bear."

Here was a perfect opportunity for Trigger's first bear dog lesson. Bears don't like dogs, and they don't like a lot of noise. Most national park literature will advise you to stand your ground, take all due precautions, and protect your food. So, with Trigger in tow, I ran over to the campsite. At first he didn't see the bear standing still behind some trees. By this time a good group of people were standing around, but no one was doing anything to chase the bear away. Now Trigger is a pretty mellow, live-and-let-live little guy (unless a person, bear or coyote is entering my campsite at nighttime) and I had to go through some pretty silly antics to get him worked up enough to even bark. I was yelling "Speak, speak! Look! Bear! Bear!" all the time waving my arms and throwing rocks. Everyone was standing around taking pictures and watching, like we were some kind of a bear chasing service. I asked some bystanders if they could throw some rocks. They said, "Oh, you want us to throw rocks too?"

Finally, the bear climbed a big tree right in the campsite where he'd stolen his dinner. Trigger and I walked through the woods to some park service residences and asked an off-duty ranger to call a bear alert patrol. The bear was still up in the tree when three rangers arrived. They waited until the bear came down and then chased him, running as fast as they could, while the bear just glanced over his shoulder and casually ambled off into the woods. It was a funny sight.

If you and your dog encounter a bear, be sure to have a tight grip on your dog and keep him close to you. Together you may be able to chase him away. Pick up a big stick if you see one, wave your arms and make lots of noise. When I talk about bears, I'm talking about the small black bears (though they can be any color) that frequent campsites. If a bear acts aggressively just back off quietly, trying to take your food with you; but it's better to lose your food rather than get into an altercation. There are not many grizzlies in the lower 48 states, but there are in Alaska and Canada. I would definitely stay out of grizzly bear country when camping with your dog. Call ahead or ask at the visitor centers if (and where) bears are a current problem.

Bears do sometimes attack dogs so always be sure the two of you are tied close so you can't be separated. When I backpacked I carried firecrackers to scare bears away. I still have them when I camp. But if you are near your car don't overlook automotive options to discourage bear vandalism, including headlights, horn, security alarm and automotive emergency flares.

If you model aggressive behavior towards bears, your dog may become inspired to bark and act aggressively. Never let your dog out of your sight in bear country because you don't want him to get the idea that he can handle it alone. Bears have killed many experienced hunting dogs that work in packs. I respect all life and I don't condone bear hunting as a sport. In my opinion, it is a senseless violent crime against nature. If a bear is truly wild, it will do its best to avoid human contact. Outside of established campgrounds where bears regularly come in close contact with people, bear vandalism is rarely a problem.

10
Without Reservation

On extended hiking and camping tours I occasionally find myself in a small, out of the way place, short of my next planned destination, but ready to stop for the night. By asking for local referrals, I have encountered some very friendly and interesting people in small towns that could only be known by word of mouth. When I know where I need to be on a particular date I will make a reservation, but otherwise my schedule is flexible.

In a small desert town in Nevada, I checked into a motel and told the couple that I had my dog in the car, and that he was a service dog, so I would not be charged a pet-cleaning fee. The woman wanted to see certification of his service dog status. I told her that under the ADA it was illegal for her to ask for that because many dogs, such as mine, are trained by their owners to meet the specific needs of those owners, and there is no national testing program to certify service dogs. She was adamantly convinced however, that she did have the right to be shown proof of certification.

The man then asked for verification of my disability and proof of why I needed a service dog. I told them that they couldn't ask for that either. The woman now decided that I was nothing but a troublemaker, and asked me to leave. She said "If you are just going to make trouble for us, we don't want your business."

I just wanted a room, without the hassle, so I said that even though it was illegal for them to ask a pet-cleaning fee for a service dog, I would pay it; but they still did not want to rent the room. The room was more important to me now than the fee, so I picked up a business card on the counter and asked if they were refusing me a room because I had a service dog. The man was angry now, and reaching for the phone he said, "Well maybe I should just call the police and we can settle this issue once and for all." I said, "Fine, but the best way for you to get information about the ADA is to call this number for the Justice Department." He called the police (who were right next door) and said, "There's this woman here, who says she has a service dog, but she won't tell us what her disability is." The police apparently declined to get involved, because they didn't come over, but the man still was not satisfied. He said "Maybe I should just go out there and see this dog for myself!" I told him that Trigger would love to meet him, and after we had settled in and gone for a little walk, I would bring him over for a visit. I said "He loves to visit with people because he is also a therapy dog. Do you know what a therapy dog is?" He said he knew all about therapy dogs because he had seen a program about that on TV. I asked if he would like to meet Trigger. At that point, there was a complete attitude adjustment. They relaxed, seemed pleased, and said they would.

After this change in attitude, I asked the couple if they would also like to learn more about the ADA. They said they would. I said: "I only have a few copies of printed material by the Justice Department about service dogs. If I left one with you would you read it with an open mind?" They said they would. So I registered for the room, got my key and we settled in. After a little walk, we stopped over for a visit. Trigger tells the rest:

"When my person came back to the car she said that she had nearly gotten us kicked out of the motel before we were even checked in. But when I got there the people were really glad to see me. I sat close to them while they talked about their little dog that died last month when a visiting dog attacked him in the parking lot. After this bad experience, I think they just had to be reminded that most of us dogs are sociable and have a lot of love to share with people. Mom told them about a favorite dog she had before she got me, and that if she had it to do over again she wouldn't have waited so long for me. I sat close while they petted me for a long time. I know they missed their little dog, and I think Mom and I did our part to encourage them to get a new little dog friend in their lives. The humans talked. I just listened."

11

Trigger's Reflections

My person says she goes to places like Yosemite and the Grand Canyon for the VIEWS, but it's hard for a dog to understand how she could be looking so far in the distance when there are so many things up close and personal to explore.

I have seen lots of animals near where I live- horses, deer, elk, squirrels, chipmunks, rabbits, turkeys; I thought I had seen them all. But when I was on my pack trip in Yosemite I saw the fattest, ugliest cat I have ever seen. Mom said it wasn't a cat, it was a MARMOT. It sat there, kept on eating, and just watched me go by. I didn't mean it any harm, but at least it could have looked worried.

Then there are those little critters that are all over the meadows (Belding ground squirrel). They just pop up out of the ground or sit on top of rocks and whistle at me as I go by; I mean, really!

I heard one in the ground under a big rock; and while I had my nose in its burrow it came out from behind the rock, climbed up on top of it, and was looking <u>down</u> on me! Mom said that looked pretty funny, and I think they were just as curious about me as I was about them.

She knows how I hate leashes. One morning we were on a potty walk and I wanted to play. I shook my leash so hard that my collar came off. (Yes, I can slip my collar, but I hardly ever do. Mom says it's a good idea in case I ever get in a tight spot and she's not there to help me.) Anyway, I caught the collar in my mouth, stayed pressed by her side, and <u>spit</u> (as best as dogs can spit) it out in her hand. "This is what I think of leashes." I was trying to say. Mom laughed, and said I was a CHARACTER, but put the collar and leash back on me. She said she still trusted me, but it was a people thing, and I was lucky to be there *with* a leash.

But once we were struggling up this very rocky and steep (3000 feet in about five miles) trail, and into a series of steep, tight switchbacks. It was hard for me to get traction on the smooth boulders, especially with the weight I was carrying. I would come to the end of my leash and slip backward before I could find a level spot. We were both getting pretty tired and discouraged. I needed to scramble and Mom needed to go slow and careful. It was my job to get her up the trail, and I wasn't doing too well. Finally she realized that if we were going to get to the next camp safe and sound, and before dark, we were going to have to do something different. So she folded my leash, tied it to my pack and sent me ahead of her the way I usually do, going up hill. Then I didn't get so tired and could turn to encourage her with a wag of my tail and a smile, "C'mon, you can do this." And she did!

The mules in the Grand Canyon haven't seen too many dogs and I'm supposed to hide if I can, when we see them coming. Once, when we saw the mules coming there was no place for me to hide close to the trail. The only possible place for me to go was down into a steep ravine between two legs of a tight switchback. Mom couldn't go down there with me, but she tied my leash to my pack and sent me down, putting me on a "down stay" with a hand signal. The mules, not more than ten feet above, surrounded me as they made their way around the switchback. I was worried, but I didn't move until Mom called me up out of the ravine after all the mules had passed. Some of the people on the mules told mom what a good dog I was, and I got treats when I came up. It's not too bad when the mules keep moving, but I really get nervous when they all stop and <u>stare</u> at me. (See Chapter Seven)

Everywhere we went, the camp staff had heard about me from the park service, and they wanted to meet me. People we passed said, "Hi Trigger, how are you?" Some of them missed their pets at home and wanted to pet me. I made a special friend with Laura, ten years old, who wanted to give me her bacon from breakfast. Mom let her give me my breakfast outside that morning, and take me for a little walk around the camp. Laura missed her Golden Retriever. Mom said I had become a CELEBRITY. They called her "Mrs. Trigger" and "Trigger's Mom," but she didn't care. She said I was a good AMBASSADOR for what we were doing.

We got the weirdest question from a man we met when we were on the trail coming down from Wheeler Peak in Great Basin National Park. He looked at me and asked my Mom: "Is he something special, or just a mutt?" I know I'm special, because Mom tells me so; but I don't know what it means to be a mutt. Mom said I was most likely a shepherd mix, and she said, "And yes, he's something special!"

12

The Search Continues

About a year after I obtained my Golden Access Passport at Crater Lake National Park I was returning to my car from a cross country ski tour on the rim road around Crater Lake when I was stopped, questioned and warned by a Ranger for having my dog with me. She entered a report on her computer. I asked for a copy of the report and a copy of the new regulations she said were in place regarding service dogs in national parks. She said no domestic animals would be allowed in the backcountry. I explained that my dog was a service/pack dog and showed her my Golden Access Passport to verify that I physically qualified for the assistance of a pack dog. She said "Anyone can get that", and that regulations were being changed to disallow all domestic animals from national parks, but that I could have a llama, if I wanted. (Thanks, I always wanted a llama!) She said they had a new superintendent and management had been changed. I would not be allowed in the backcountry with my service dog.

When I talked to Tom Coleman in National Park Administration Services he said he was not aware of any such rule and they were still working on the verbiage of the rule to include access for all service dogs in their CFRs. After talking to Tom Coleman I wrote a letter to my Congressman and Representative (see appendix). Shortly after that I got confirmation that the issue would be investigated, and I left on a six-week tour of national parks in the Southwest.

About a week into my trip I stopped at a brand new visitor center in Zion to talk to a park superintendent or a corridor ranger and give my letter of introduction and notify them of my intent to walk on trails with my pack dog. The visitor center was so new it was not yet opened (although the sign said it was), so I gave my letter to a ranger I saw outside. He said I could not hike with my dog on a trail, and the only service dogs allowed on trails were "seeing eye" (guide) dogs and "hearing ear" (sound alert) dogs. I told him that the National Park's CFRs (Code of Federal Regulations) were out of compliance with the ADA (Americans with Disabilities Act) and that the ADA took precedence over any other law, unless that law was less restrictive than the ADA. He said that if I took Trigger on a trail with me I would be cited. I said, "Well let them cite me and then we'll find out whose right!" He advised me to go over to the old visitor center and talk to someone there. I said, "I'm giving you this notice explaining my background, my dog's training, my intentions, and information numbers where you can find out more about the ADA. Please pass this on to the appropriate person and if anyone wants to talk to me, I'll be in campsite number 7, South Campground, after 4 PM this afternoon." He asked what trails I would be hiking. I said, "I don't know, but since it is hot, probably short ones; and the dog might not even be wearing a pack." Because he is a service dog he can accompany me wherever I go whether he is actually working as a service dog at that moment, or not.

I asked my traveling companion if I was assertive enough. Long pause. Then, "I hope so." No one came to talk to me, not that I really expected them to. But since that conversation I have decided it's OK to just wait until I am approached by a ranger on the trail, rather than go to all the visitor centers when I arrive. I always carry a copy of my letter of introduction with me, just in case I am stopped, but since this incident I am being questioned less and less as time goes by.

The next national park I visited after this encounter at Zion was Bryce. I told the camp host couple what I was doing (I thought they were rangers as they had look alike uniforms), and I gave them a copy of my letter. He said I should clear it with the corridor ranger, but being a little weary of talking to rangers about my intentions, I didn't go back to the visitor center again that afternoon. The camp hosts were a fun couple to talk to, and for the most part supportive. She even offered to take care of Trigger while I was hiking, but of course he came with me.

While I was walking the rim trail at Bryce that evening there was a big group of German tourists who just cracked up at the sight of Trigger's "Service Dog" patch on his pack. I don't know what <u>service dog</u> means in German, but one of the men asked what kind of services he performed, and another, clutching his chest, asked if he had something for his heart. I said "No, no brandy." And that was all they needed to set them off in gales of laughter again. They were having a great time.

I have pondered for months why they thought Trigger's <u>service dog</u> patch was so funny, and I think I finally have the answer. In Europe dogs accompany their people everywhere, including restaurants. Everyone knows that dogs are friends, helpers, and part of the family. There is no need to <u>label</u> them as something special because there are no restrictions on where any of them can go. So, if a dog is labeled for everyone to see, the dog must be there to perform some kind of public service. *Now* I get it.

It was fun to listen to all the comments about a pack dog on the trail. Many people spoke to him in a variety of accents and languages, and most people expressed pleasure in seeing him. And then an amazing thing happened. As two park rangers approached, I thought, "Oh boy, here we go again." I was ready to introduce myself and explain why I had a right to be there. But they gave me big, broad smiles, nodded, and just walked right on past. I couldn't believe they didn't say anything. Then I passed them again going the other way and they smiled and nodded again, as if to say "It's OK." Incredible! That was the turning point, and from then on it was a lot easier.

I even got a politically correct question at a national monument I visited as I went through the entrance station: "Is this pet your assistance dog"? Wow, it was almost as if they were expecting me. Technically service dogs aren't pets, but Trigger doesn't know that, and they can call him a pet if they want to. It's just so nice to be greeted with an open question. And since then, as I made my way through various national parks I have had conversations with rangers who openly acknowledge the intrinsic value of dogs as traveling companions.

I am very pleased to report that as this book is going to press, there is new legislation that has been introduced into Title 36, Section 2.15 that will allow ALL service dogs access in backcountry of national parks. You can view the Code of Federal Regulations on line. See *Resources* in the appendix for the URL.

It is important to recognize here that it was the diligent work and dedication of a few people in Washington D. C. that provided the education, support and encouragement to make this undertaking possible. And I could not have done it without the help of many people along the way.

13

Where Do You Get a Pack Dog?

It's not as simplistic an answer as my three-year-old granddaughter gave me when she said she wanted a lion for Christmas. When asked where she thought we could get a lion, she knew exactly where: "Well, you just go to the jungle store!"

So then, where do you get a good pack dog? Say you are starting out with a puppy that is going to be large enough to carry a pack, healthy, confidently assertive, and apparently willing to please. Hopefully you have already given this project some serious thought and you willingly and joyfully accept the role of parent, guardian, teacher, leader, partner, and friend for life. You have acquired a brand new little being with lots of energy who is ready to explore his very own brand new world!

So what do you do next, besides the obvious routine of feeding, exercise and housebreaking? Is it about training? I would say no, especially from the puppy's point of view. It's more about shaping desirable behaviors and managing his learning experiences. The important thing is that time together should be fun for both you and the puppy. He should be set up for successes so that he can be praised and rewarded.

If a puppy is going to develop into a secure and confident outdoor dog he needs to spend a lot of time in an outdoor environment. If hiking and camping are already part of your lifestyle, including your new puppy will just make it that much more fun. Trails, campgrounds and parks are his classroom and his playground. Give him plenty of time to explore his surroundings. Let him stop and "smell the roses." He needs to find out as much as he can about other animals because he will be meeting a lot of them. Keep him close to you, on a leash at all times at first. Have him sit beside you when he is watching a squirrel or a deer and seems tempted to run. Pet and praise him for maintaining a steady sit while observing other animals, kids, dogs, bicycles, horses, or llamas—and any other animals to which you can think to introduce him.

Spend time with him at horse shows, county fairs and dog shows. Let lots of people pet him. Go to pet fairs, fund-raisers and parades for pets. The more exposure your puppy gets to all this activity the more confidence he will have as an adult, and the more dependable he will be in public. That is assuming you introduce him gradually and at a distance to all this activity. You don't want to frighten him or overload his puppy senses.

There is an ideal time in canine development to give him all these guided experiences. And since they will make a very deep and lasting impression you want them all to be positive and fun. Less than four months is the age when he is most dependent on you, so it is an ideal time to teach him that the safe, secure and rewarding place for him to be is at your side. Make it worth his while to look at you frequently for praise and lots of treats. Train before meals so that he is hungry. You don't want him to find out how much fun it would be to chase after a squirrel or a dog. However, I never scold or try to divert his attention when he is looking at other animals. He can look all he wants, he just has to stay close to me. If he pulls at the leash I make him sit. Gradually you should be getting voluntary and automatic sits when other animals or people are around. Work toward using the leash less for restraint and more just for backup.

Just as important as exposure is to all this stimuli is the free time to play and interact with other puppies and dogs. Set up play dates with people and neighbors you know who have friendly dogs. After all his puppy shots take him to dog parks or anyplace he can safely socialize with his own kind. Supervise these interactions carefully if he is still at a very young and impressionable age. Playing is learning. If he is going to be confident and secure he needs to know how to get along with other dogs. Dogs that have not been adequately socialized with other dogs are more apt to be dog aggressive, fearful, or become nuisance barkers.

Try to anticipate all the common nuisance behaviors that are likely to get your dog into trouble. Now is the time to insure against them before they become habits. When a neighbor dog chases a car, or barks at someone walking down the street, before my dog is tempted to follow this example I give him a tasty treat. Pretty soon my dog expects a treat every time the dog across the street misbehaves. And this is a very good thing. You want your dog to look to you at times of distraction and temptation because you don't want him to find out that it would be fun to chase. You want to provide a greater or more rewarding experience for him, such as a game of tug, a favorite toy (saved for training rewards), or a food treat. Gradually you can reduce and eliminate these reward incentives as the temptation subsides.

If you have been walking and working with your puppy every day, by the time he is five or six months old he has learned a lot, and hopefully it has all been fun and games for the puppy. You have gone to great efforts to protect him from any kind of traumatic experience in his most vulnerable months, and you are shaping his responses to common stimuli in the outdoors. You are helping him to explore and make sense of his world by allowing him to stop and listen to sounds, and smell where people and animals have been. You allow him to observe everything. There is a lot of information to process, and he is working on it. He knows he can count on you for guidance and he is secure in his pack position with you as his protector and leader.

By the time you are ready for more structured training your puppy will probably be way ahead of other puppies in your class because you two have a special bond, and your dog is already looking to you for direction. And even though you have some challenging times ahead when your puppy goes through a brief "teenager" phase, you now have the management tools and skills to get you through it. Wild canines must start to fend for themselves when they are approaching adulthood, and the instinct to pull away and become independent is still strong in some domesticated dogs. (You did choose a confident and adventurous dog, didn't you?) Knowing that this is just a normal and necessary phase will help to reduce the frustration that you may feel when your friend impulsively decides that he knows all that he needs to know now, and is ready to go out and meet the world on his own. Just reinforce your leadership role by making him work more for treats, food and petting. Keep him on a leash all the time, if you don't already. If your male dog has not yet been neutered, now would be a good time to do it. But most of all, keep it in perspective; you will soon be back to normal. Fortunately, the teenage phase is measured in weeks for dogs, not in years.

I guess you know by now what makes a great trail dog, because you have just laid the foundation for one! But up until now, the dog didn't really have much to do with it.

14

What Makes a Good Team?

A dog left to his own devices is just a dog. On his own he will just do what he has to do to survive. If he doesn't have a leader, he will either look for one or form his own pack. So far it is only your intention that because you chose him, he will be a great trail dog. You are giving him the opportunity to follow you everywhere. But will he?

What is the nebulous and almost mystical ingredient that makes a dog special? What is it that inspires a dog (or a person) to greatness? Some things come to my mind; others may come to yours:

Someone who believes in them

Permission to make some mistakes while learning

Unconditional acceptance of one's intrinsic worth

Great trail (pack) dogs don't just happen. After socialization and shaping, the single most important factor is the working relationship that you and your dog will develop. The bond that you have formed is based on trust, understanding and the willingness to please. You have worked hard to give your dog the positive experiences he needs to develop good judgment. But a dog can only be great if he has a great partner to rely on. The only true test of this bond is how you respect, understand, and relate to each other. How would your dog rate you on a scale of one to ten as his leader? Ever been scored by a dog before? Humbling thought, isn't it? The true/false questionnaire might look something like this:

> Generally, I know what is expected of me and I have a secure place in my pack.
>
> I know my needs will be met because I have a daily routine I can count on.
>
> I don't have to bark a lot to get the attention I need.
>
> I spend a lot of time with my pack, both indoors and out.
>
> I clearly always know when I have pleased my person.

Sometimes I get rewarded for doing nothing (like not barking or chasing cars)

On a sit-stay I can't wait to run to my person because something good or fun usually happens.

When I am called and come right away, my person often lets me run free again to play.

When I am distracted and don't come right away my person doesn't nag me or get angry. He or she comes to me and puts my leash on and we walk back to the car.

As a team you are starting to understand and respect each other's strengths and weaknesses. Make clear and maintain your ultimate leadership with compassion and balance. When you can't lead with assurance, trust enough to follow. The alpha pack member doesn't always lead the pack. As a team you will learn how to work together, read each other's body language, recognize and acknowledge non-verbal signals, messages and feelings. Know when to take charge and when to follow.

When things go wrong don't blame the dog. Take a step or two back in your training progression and reinforce what the dog already knows. Don't damage your relationship by resorting to negative training methods. The dog won't be as willing to try new behaviors and take initiative if you use fear-based tactics. Remember—you started with a confident and willing partner and you want to preserve that attitude at all costs. He may have a lapse in judgment or be downright naughty on occasion, but if your relationship is sound, he really does want to please you!

Start giving your dog some easy self-initiating tasks, such as "Go to the car." When you have left the trail and are ready to go back teach your dog "Go to the trail." Or, after more formalized retrieval training say something like "I dropped my keys. Would you go find them for me please?" (You have set this up by quietly placing the keys in the middle of the trail while the dog is ahead of you). A precursor to this was a "hide-the-cookie" game that we played at home. Then a toy was substituted for the cookie and traded for the reward. Then we used the keys instead of a toy. Now he eagerly finds and brings me the keys no matter where we are.

Your responsibility as a guardian is to encourage and teach your dog to become the most he can be. His responsibility to you is to offer to take charge when he knows his senses are stronger than yours.

With some training and sense of direction dogs will happily participate in all kinds of adventures with their human families.

These signals will be subtle but learn to read them. Keep him on a leash or dragline at first, and give him lots of praise and encouragement. Your responsibility to each other is to always know where your partner is and what he or she is doing. I used to hide occasionally from Trigger when I could catch him off guard. But either I'm getting a lot slower or he is getting a lot smarter because I can't get hidden anymore before he runs up to me.

Does a dog take responsibility because it is inherent in his nature, or because he is trusted and encouraged to act on his intuition? Probably both. But there are all degrees of comfort levels in this kind of a relationship. It is up to each team to find its own level.

15

Visiting National Parks With Dogs

Legally, there is a clear distinction between a service dog and a pet. Dogs, as pets, are strictly limited where they can go in a national park. Official park regulations prohibit pets in all areas of the park except "developed areas" as defined in 36 CFR, Section 1.4, which states:

> "Developed area means roads, parking areas, picnic areas, campgrounds, or other structures, facilities or lands located within development and historic zones depicted on the park area land management and use map."

However, consider this "friendly reminder" that I was handed as I went through the entrance station of one national park:

Dogs must be on a leash at all times.

Dogs are not allowed on any trails.

You can only walk your dog on paved areas.

Do not leave your dog unattended at any time.

Do not leave your dog locked up in your vehicle.

Some national parks and monuments also prohibit tying your dog to a fixed object. Beginning to sound like a catch twenty-two? Each park superintendent can make exceptions to the uniform code, and the regulations can vary widely from park to park. Some allow dogs on trails adjacent to roads and on short paved access trails to points of interest close to roads. In national parks, with few exceptions, dogs (as pets) are not allowed in the backcountry, and the definition of backcountry is subject to change with the season. In Crater Lake National Park the rim road around Crater Lake is a developed area when the road is drivable, but when closed by snow it becomes backcountry.

Often, a person traveling with a dog does not have any options for getting off of a road or out of a campground. More and more paved and dirt roads that were open to vehicles (and therefore open to dogs) are being closed and designated as trails. Dog owners are not supposed to walk on these converted roads either. While I resent that choosing to travel with a dog (as a pet) severely limits where I can go, I do understand the need to regulate and control the great masses of people who visit our national parks.

I met a man jogging in Red Rock Canyon in Nevada (not a national park) accompanied by a large German Shepherd and a Doberman, both off leash. Trigger was on a leash because that was the requirement. I passed the trio and the Dobie turned back to follow me, not heeding the man's "come" command. I stopped and waited for the man to come back and get a hold of his dog. I couldn't believe what happened next. Because the Dobie was on the other side of Trigger, he bodily picked Trigger up by the skin on his back and tossed him aside so he could get a hold of his dog. It is this kind of thoughtless and rude behavior that causes all dog owners to gradually lose off leash privileges on public lands.

When I go camping in a national park the first thing I have to be concerned about is my dog's safety and well being. If he isn't used to being tied out and left alone for more than a few minutes at a time, then I shouldn't leave him alone. When a dog is insecure and unsupervised the owner is especially vulnerable to criticism and possible citation. And a dog doesn't have to be left alone to be unsupervised. Some people ignore their dogs when they are in the campsite and their dog is barking at other park visitors. If we want to bring our dogs to public campgrounds we should train them (from the time they are puppies) to ignore normal foot traffic and other dogs close by.

While my first responsibility is to my dog, my second responsibility is to the people that I meet along the way and those that will follow me later. Did I check the campsite to make sure it was clean when I left? Did I toilet my dog where people don't walk? Striving for consistency with good training and hygiene habits, to leave people with good impressions about dogs in national parks, may not always conform to the well-intentioned park regulations.

Even camp hosts and rangers in the same national park aren't always consistent with regulations regarding the walking of pets in a specific campground. In Bryce, our first camp host said it was OK to walk dogs off road, anywhere within the campground. Her alternate camp host said dogs could only be walked on the roads. So on my next trip to the visitor center I asked a ranger what the rule was and she said it was "a gray area", and asked another ranger. I asked what the CFRs said about pets in campgrounds, and I got a copy of the rules and the definition of a developed area (see above). The rules go on to state:

> "All visitors will be responsible for
> disposing of pet excrement in the

following areas: all parking areas, picnic and campgrounds and the area around Camper Store, Lodge, Nature Center and Visitor Center. Excrement must be disposed of by placing it in the adjacent woods or bushes at least 35 feet from any of these developed areas, or by placing excrement in a closed disposable bag in a garbage container. "

My question would be "If my dog has to be with me at all times, and I have to deposit his excrement in the adjacent woods, why can't he just *deposit* it there himself?"

However, either each park superintendent has a lot of latitude in the setting of rules, or no one is held accountable for abiding by the definition of *developed area*, because in many parks, dogs are excluded from areas that appear to be very *developed*, such as an outdoor amphitheater within a campground, and cement sidewalks leading to rest rooms.

When you camp with your dog in national parks your concepts of good stewardship may be challenged, so be prepared to make some difficult decisions.

16

Future of Dog Packing in National Parks

Is there a future for dog packing in national parks? There could be, if people traveling with dogs in national parks show consideration and respect for other visitors.

In the Grand Canyon on the North Kaibab Trail I met a mule driver who singled me out of a group of hikers standing off the trail waiting for the mules to pass. "You, the woman with the dog, do you know pets are not allowed on the trail?" "Yes I do. This is not a pet, it's a service dog." She continued, "Well I want to be sure he won't bark at my mules." "No, he won't bark at the mules." Trigger meanwhile is lying down well off the trail in the shade, with his eyes half closed and his head between his paws. He hasn't even flicked an ear at the presence of the mules. (He's an old *paw* at this mule thing now.) After more questioning, doubts, and drawn out speculations I said, "Look, the mules know my dog is here, but he isn't going to do anything but lie there until you pass." Trigger didn't move, as I'm sure he was glad for the rest.

After they passed, one young man gave me a broad grin and a thumbs-up, and said, "I really like the way you handled that woman." And others in the group agreed and wished me a great day. Well, I don't know what I said that was so great, but I do know this: There is a whole lot of support out there, from the hiking public, for dog packing.

If there was an organization to promote dog packing, maybe dog owners could reach a consensus on what it is we want and work toward educating ourselves and the public as to what we expect of ourselves. What is our part of the bargain? What kind of privileges would we like to earn? Hiking with a dog (as a pet) in a national park should be an earned privilege, not a right. Even as Trigger must earn the privilege to be off leash where leashes are not required, so must I and other dog owners take more responsibility for their supervision and control, especially in high use areas.

What kind of training should the dog have?

Should there be a certification process for non-service dogs?

What kind of an agreement should the owner sign?

Should there be a performance test for the human/canine team?

Who should issue the certification or conduct the test?

How would such an organization establish and maintain credibility?

I have talked to people from all over the world, and from all parts of the U.S. Not because I travel widely, but because I visit a lot of national parks. Trigger and I (as a team) are magnets for people who have dogs at home and would like to hike with them. A lot of people would like to see some kind of special permit program for those of us who like to hike with our dogs.

Considering the established tradition of pack carrying domestic animals (with mules and llamas being allowed) is it so much of a stretch of the imagination to allow that trained pack dogs could also perform this needed function?

If we as dog owners want to work towards that possibility we have to actively educate ourselves and others about canine trail manners and regulate dog packing so as to minimize the risk of losing what freedoms we still have. Many other users of public lands have organizations to promote their interests. Dog owners do not have any real national voice, or lobbying group; but yet there are a lot of dog owners who would like to be considered as fair share users of public lands.

So if you have occasion to visit national parks with your best friend remember—you are on stage center front all the time. You are setting an example, good or bad, for all those who would like to follow. Trigger and I have done our best to set a good one.

Bibliography and Resources

Getting Started:

Hall, Adrienne. *Backpacking: A Woman's Guide*. Blacklick, OH: Ragged Mountain Press, Mcgraw Hill, 1998. Equipment, fitness, and safety techniques.

Seaborg, Eric, and Ellen Dudley. *Hiking and Backpacking*. Champaign, IL: Human Kinetics Publishers, 1994. Introduction to backpacking.

Backpacking Skills and Techniques:

Berger, Karen. *Everyday Wisdom: 1001 Expert Tips for Hikers*. Seattle, WA: The Mountaineers, 1997. Expert tips on all aspects of backpacking.

Berger, Karen. *Hiking and Backpacking: A Complete Guide*. New York, NY: W.W. Norton and Co., 1995. A "how to" trail guide on specific techniques.

Curtis, Rick. *The Backpacker's Field Manual.* New York, NY: Crown Publishing Group, 1997. Basic survival, planning, first aid, safety and emergencies.

Fleming, June. *Staying Found.* Seattle, WA: The Mountaineers, 1994. Orienteering.

Ross, Cindy and Todd Gladfelter. *A Hiker's Companion.* Seattle, WA: The Mountaineers, 1993. Food planning, improvising, and basic survival skills.

Townsend, Chris. *The Backpacker's Handbook.* Camden, ME: Ragged Mountain Press, McGraw Hill, 1996. Clothing and shelter for extreme conditions.

Dogs and Backpacking:

Labelle, Charleen. *A Guide to Backpacking With Your Dog.* Loveland, CO: Alpine Publications, 1993. Dog pack selection, packing, care and training, public lands.

Lerner, Richard. *Hiking With Your Dog.* Mukilteo, WA.: Alpenbooks, 1994. Written by a veterinarian

Richmond and Barash. *Ruffing It*. Loveland, CO: Alpine Publications, 1999. Complete and thoughtful guide to dog-packing

Smith, Cheryl. *On the Trail with Your Canine Companion*. New York, NY: Howell Book House, Simon and Schuster, Macmillan Co., 1996. A thoughtful discussion of all aspects of camping and hiking with your dog.

Dogs and Nature:

Mills, Enos and Kent Dannen. *The Story of Scotch*. Loveland, CO: Alpine Publications, 1998.Enos Mills was the founder of Rocky Mountain National Park

Muir, John as retold by Donnel Rubay. *Stickeen*. Nevada City, CA: Dawn Publications, 1998. Muir, father of the environmental movement tells the story of his exploration of Alaska with his dog friend.

Dog Training

Fisher, John. *Think Dog*. North Pomfret, Vermont: Trafalgar Square Publishing, 1991. An owner's guide to canine psychology

Miller, Pat. *The Power of Positive Dog Training*. New York, NY: John Wiley and Sons, 2001. Leading proponent of positive dog training.

Pryor, Karen. *Don't Shoot the Dog*. New York, NY: Simon Schuster and Schuster, 1984. Training and behavior modification.

Wild Canines:

Lopez, Barry. *Of Wolves and Men*. Scribner, Simon and Schuster, New York, N.Y.1978. A classic in-depth study of canine ancestry and a history of their human associations.

RESOURCES

Access Specialist, National Park Service, Park Facility Management Division. 1201 Eye NW (2420), Washington DC, 20005. (202) 513-7031 Info on service dogs in national parks.

Americans With Disabilities Act Disability Rights Section, Civil Rights Division, U.S. Department of Justice, P.O. Box 66738, Washington, D.C. 20035-6738. (800) 514-0301 (voice), (800) 514-0383 (TDD) www.usdoj.gov/crt/ada

Canine Good Citizen Program, The American Kennel Club. 5580 Centerview Dr., Suite 200,Raleigh, NC 27606. www.akc.org/love/cgc. Order a free information kit.

Code of Federal Regulations, home page: http://www.access.gpo.gov/nara/cfr/, or Title 36, Parks, Forests and Public Property: http://www.access.gpo.gov/nara/cfr/waisid x_02/36cfr2_02.html

Cross Country Publications: crosscountrypublications.com. Links to most resource websites listed here.

Delta Society, 580 Naches Ave. SW, Suite
101, Renton, WA 98055-2297; (425)
226-7357. www.deltasociety.org. Mission
is to improve human health through
service and therapy animals. One of their
goals is to remove barriers that prevent
involvement of animals in every day life.

Doctors Foster & Smith. (800) 826-7206.
www.DrsFosterSmith.com. Pet products
catalog. (No minimum order)

Muttluks, Inc. (888) 688-8585.
www.muttluks.com. All weather dog boot
is available.

The Whole Dog Journal. (800) 829-9165 (to
subscribe). 1117 Regent St., Alameda, CA
94501. www.WholeDogJ@aol.com. A
monthly guide to natural dog care and
positive training.

Wind River Bear Institute. P.O. Box 307,
Heber City, UT 84032.
www.beardogs.org

Wolf Packs, LLC. 755 Tyler Creek Rd.,
Ashland, OR 97520-9408. (541) 482-
7669. www.wolfpacks.com. Dog packs
and dog packing info.

Letter To Senator Gordon Smith

April 4, 2000
Senator Gordon Smith
121 SW Salmon, Suite 1250
Portland, OR 97204

Dear Senator Smith:

About two and a half years ago I petitioned the National
Park Service to allow me the use of my service/pack dog on
trails in the backcountry of national parks. At that time
the NPS was in the process of revising its Code of Federal
Regulations to more accurately reflect the intentions of the
Americans With Disabilities Act. The Access Specialist I
talked to at that time advised me to apply for a Golden
Access Passport (which I did) and said that when I showed
that to superintendents of national parks I should be
allowed the use of my service/pack dog on trails where pets
are prohibited.

On Feb. 18th of this year I had just returned to my vehicle
from a short cross country ski tour on the rim road around
Crater Lake. I was warned by a ranger that dogs were not
allowed in the back country. I explained that my dog was a
service/pack dog and showed her my Golden Access
Passport to verify that I physically qualified for the
assistance of a pack dog. She said "Anyone can get that",
and that regulations were being changed to disallow all
domestic animals from national parks.

I would expect by now, the Code of Federal Regulations
would show compliance with the intentions of the ADA.
As you know, the Department of Justice does not handle
ADA complaints against the Federal

Government. Would I have to file a complaint with GSA Agencies Office of Disability in Washington DC, with the same agent who has been acting as my advocate? This office is well aware of the problems involved with implementing compliance with Sec. 504 of the Rehabilitation Act of 1973.

How can anyone enforce compliance of a law when the official regulations for that law are not yet written? And isn't going back to the same agency to enforce compliance of itself a lot like asking the fox to guard the henhouse? In all fairness to the park staff, how can they be expected to enforce any kind of uniform disability rights policy when all they have to work with are rumors and promises of regulations not yet written?

Is there anything you can do to expedite a uniform disability rights policy within the National Park Service?

Respectfully,

Jane G. Cox

Letter From Senator Gordon Smith

GORDON H. SMITH
OREGON

COMMITTEES:
BUDGET
ENERGY AND NATURAL RESOURCES
FOREIGN RELATIONS

United States Senate
WASHINGTON, DC 20510-3704

May 31, 2000

Ms. Jane G. Cox
241 Manzanita
Prospect, OR 97536

Dear Ms. Cox:

It is a pleasure to be able to supply you with the enclosed information from the U.S Department of the Interior's National Park Service, which I received in response to my inquiry on your behalf. I hope this information will be helpful to you.

Thank you for taking the time to contact me. Please let me know if you have any questions or feel I can be of further assistance with any other federally related matter.

Sincerely,

Gordon H. Smith
United States Senator

GHS:mh
Enclosure

95

Response from National Park Service

United States Department of the Interior

NATIONAL PARK SERVICE
1849 C Street, N.W.
Washington, D.C. 20240

IN REPLY REFER TO:

A36(2420)

MAY 2 5 2000

Honorable Gordon H. Smith
United States Senator
One World Trade Center
121 SW Salmon Street
Suite 1250
Portland, Oregon 97204

Dear Senator Smith:

Thank you for your letter of April 25, 2000, on behalf of your constituent, Ms. Jane Cox. Ms. Cox is asking for clarification on National Park Service (NPS) policies and regulations regarding the use of service animals by individuals with disabilities. Ms. Cox is particularly concerned about the acceptance of service dogs for individuals with mobility impairments, and the need to ensure consistent administration of this policy throughout the NPS.

In 1990, with the passage of the American's with Disabilities Act (ADA), Congress broadened the concept of service dogs for blind and hearing impaired individuals to include animals that provide a service for other disability groups, including pack animals for individuals with mobility limitations. Even though the ADA does not technically apply to Federal agencies, the NPS has recognized the intent of Congress and has taken steps to officially amend our regulations accordingly. We are currently taking steps to expedite the completion of a number of regulations, including the one related to the use of service animals. In the interim, we will issue a directive to our parks advising them of the broadened definition of service animals. This should result in the clarification and consistency that Ms. Cox is seeking.

The NPS Accessibility Management Program is responsible for guiding our efforts with regard to providing the highest level of access that is practicable for people with disabilities, in conformance with Federal rules and regulations.

If you or your constituent would like more specific information, please contact Mr. David Park 202/565-1255 or Mr. Tom Coleman at 202/565-1256.

Sincerely,

Maureen Finnerty
Associate Director, Park Operations
and Education

Copy to your Washington, D.C., office

96

Letter to *Wildlife Biologist, Yosemite (excerpted)*

Nov. 25, 1998

About a month ago I was one of your 1000 people this
year who experienced bear break-in to my camper van.
Had I been told upon entering the park I was at high risk
for a bear attack on my vehicle I would not have stayed in
the park after dark. I was at high risk because I cook and
eat in my van when I travel.

The glass company in Merced say they are replacing more
glass from bear break-ins in Yosemite than ever this year,
and by your own admission the problem is getting worse.
Bear incidents of 900 and rising is not a statistic of which
to be proud.

Just telling people that you had 900 bear break-ins last
year does not absolve you of responsibility to control the
problem. A flyer that you hand people at the gate is too
little too late. The first thing on a visitor's mind is finding
a place to stay, and I didn't even have time to look at your
guide and materials till the next day. Now I know that the
next time I leave a vehicle in Yosemite over night it will be
a rental vehicle, not my own.

I think that a vehicle profile assessment at the gate would
be helpful to prevent incidents. Since the first concern
visitors have on entering the park is where they will spend
the night, park staff could be a lot more helpful in this
area. Had I been able to park in an overflow campground
my vehicle would not have been unattended. Lacking that
possibility with a converted van I probably should have

been advised not to stay in the park. I think it is irresponsible of the park service to take

entrance fees when campsites are full or intentionally unavailable; and when there are no minimally protected areas for vehicles at high risk to park.

The bears are empowered to take whatever they want with no consequences. Their experience at Yosemite has taught them that they are at the top of the food chain. So if the bears are going to go back to foraging for "natural" food it is up to humans to restore their "natural" fear of people.

There must be more you can do to prevent and discourage bear damage. With 25 years of research and $500,000 in federal funding each year you must have learned a lot about bear behavior. And there is a wealth of new information on animal behavior and aversive conditioning in general.

I know I am not alone when I say that nothing would make me happier than to know that bears have been restored to their natural rightful place in the wild with a healthy respect for human life and property. I would also like to get new information as it becomes available on your bear management program in Yosemite.

Very truly yours,

Jane G. Cox

Golden Access Passport

for Persons Who are Blind or Permanently Disabled

What Is It?

The Golden Access Passport is a lifetime entrance pass to most national parks, monuments, historic sites, recreation areas, and national wildlife refuges that charge an entrance fee.

The Golden Access Passport admits the pass holder and any accompanying passengers in a private vehicle. Where entry is not by private vehicle, the passport admits the pass holder, spouse, and children.

The Golden Access Passport also provides a 50% discount on federal use fees charged for facilities and services such as camping, swimming, parking, boat launching, and cave tours.[1] It does not cover or reduce special recreation permit fees or fees charged by concessioners.[2]

How do I get one?

A Golden Access Passport **MUST** be obtained **IN PERSON** at any federal area where an entrance fee is charged or at one of the agencies listed in this pamphlet. It is available only to citizens or permanent residents of the United States who have been medically determined to be blind or permanently disabled. You may obtain a Golden Access Passport by showing proof of medically determined permanent disability or eligibility for receiving benefits under federal law.

[1] In some cases where use fees are charged, the pass holder only will be given the 50% reduction; for example, cave tours, elevator services, or group camping.
[2] The Forest Service requires private concession operators of federally owned campgrounds on national forest lands to provide a 50% discount in the recreation use fee to Golden Age Passport holders.

The National Park Service's Golden Access Passport (GAP) that addresses needs of Park Visitors with disabilities (no form number or date).

Wrong side of loop Velcro® facing up when boot is right side out

Loop Velcro® is sewn into seam so that it can be wrapped
<u>behind</u> the leg and then over the hook part in front.
Pattern includes ½ inch seam allowance and is for about
a sixty or seventy pound dog. Seam can be trimmed to
reduce bulk before turning.

Hook Velcro® sewn to front before sewing front
and back together

Front

(outside view)

Cut 8 pieces for 4 boots – extras come in handy

101

Index

Quick Order Form

Dog Packing in National Parks

Quantity:		
X $14.95 ea. =	$	
Shipping and handling: ($5 first, $2 ea addl)........................	$	
Total:	$	

Send to: (Name)

(Address)

(City)   (State)   (Zip)

Telephone:

Email address:

Please submit check or money order with order made out to Cross Country Publications and mail to:

Cross Country Publications
P.O. Box 3369
Central Point, OR 97502-0014

Contact by email for discounts:
crosscountrypublications@cybernetisp.net

Please allow six to eight weeks for delivery.